Why Why Why did knights wear heavy armour?

Miles
Kelly
PUBLISHING

First published in 2005 by
Miles Kelly Publishing Ltd
Bardfield Centre, Great Bardfield, Essex, CM7 4SL

2 4 6 8 10 9 7 5 3 1

Editorial Director
Belinda Gallagher

Art Director
Jo Brewer

Editorial Assistant
Amanda Askew

Author
Catherine Chambers

Volume Designer
Venita Kidwai

Indexer
Helen Snaith

Production Manager
Estela Boulton

Scanning and Reprographics
Anthony Cambray, Mike Coupe, Ian Paulyn

ISBN 1-84236-598-3

Printed in China

British Library Cataloguing-in-Publication Data
A catalogue record for this book is available
from the British Library

www.mileskelly.net
info@mileskelly.net

Contents

Why were castles built on hills?

People began building castles over 1000 years ago. They were built on a hill so that people could see the enemy better. The hill was made from a huge mound of mud and stones. It was called a motte.

Motte

Were all castles made from wood?

Early castles were made from wood. They were not very strong and they caught fire easily. People began to build stone castles. These were much stronger. They lasted longer and did not burn.

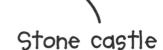

Stone castle

Slimy walls!
Builders often covered wooden castles with wet, slippery leather. This stopped them from burning so easily.

What was a moat?

Builders dug a big ditch around the castle. Then they filled it with water. This watery ditch was called a moat. Enemy soldiers got wet and cold if they attacked the castle from the moat. It was hard to fight from the bottom of it, too!

Think
Stone castles were a lot warmer in winter than wooden ones. Why do you think this was so?

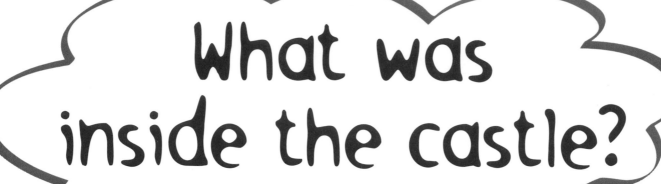

What was inside the castle?

A big courtyard was inside the castle. This was called a bailey. A thick wall was built all around it. Smaller buildings were put up inside the bailey. Sometimes there were gardens. There were often animals and chickens, too!

Thick wall

Where was the safest place?

The safest place in the castle was a tall, strong tower. This tower was called a keep. The lord of the castle lived there with his family. In later times they slept on the top floor. There were big rooms downstairs to hold feasts for visitors.

Keep

Thick walls!

The walls of the keep were at least 3.5 metres thick! This meant that building a castle took a long time. It was also a very expensive job.

Water wheel

How did people get bread and water?

A castle often had its own mill and bakery. Many castles got water from a well. The well was dug inside the bailey. A massive wheel drew water up into the castle. Later castles had piped water with taps.

Measure

The walls of the keep were 3.5 metres thick. Use a tape measure to see how thick this is.

Who was in charge of the castle?

Lady

The king controlled the castle and all the lands around it. Lords and knights worked and fought for the king. They often had their own castles. The queen or lady of the castle was in charge of everyone who worked in the castle.

Lord

It's a long way to wash!

Maids and servants went outside the castle to wash and get rid of fleas. They had to find a stream to get clean!

Steward

Cook

Servant

Who did all the work?

Many maids and servants looked after the lord of the castle. They cooked, cleaned, served dinner, ran errands and mended things. The steward was in charge of all the servants. The lady of the castle was his boss.

Be a steward

Pretend you are a castle steward. Write down all your servants' jobs for the day. Be kind to them!

Who protected the villagers?

The king controlled villages outside the castle. Enemies often attacked them. So the villagers ran to the castle for protection. They were allowed to stay in the bailey. The villagers often brought their animals, too!

Who was ruler of the land?

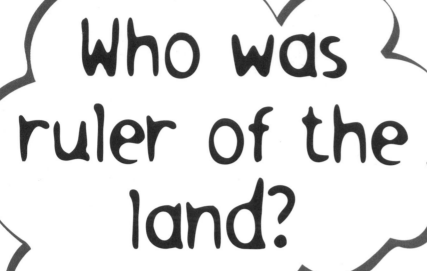

The king and queen ruled the land. Then came the barons and lords. Church leaders such as bishops were also powerful. The Church controlled large areas of land.

Draw

Draw a tree to show the most and least powerful people in the land. Put the king or queen on the top branch. Who would you draw below them?

King

Bishop

Queen

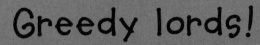

Greedy lords!

The poorest people were called peasants. Everything they owned including land, animals, food and even their clothes, belonged to the local lord.

Fighting men

Baron

Who were the barons?

The barons were the most powerful noblemen. They supplied the king with men who could fight in times of trouble. A rich baron might have 5000 fighting men. Some barons even had their own armies.

Who wanted to fight?

Knights were skilled horsemen and excellent soldiers. They fought for kings, lords and barons. These noblemen paid the knights with some of their land.

What happened at knight school?

A knight had to train for 14 years! First, he went to a lord's house when he was seven years old. There, he was taught how to ride and to shoot with a bow. Then he became a squire and was taught how to fight with a sword.

Teacher

Count

A nobleman's son went to knight school when he was seven. He studied for 14 years. How old was he when he became a knight?

Who had the best horses?

Rich knights owned three horses. The heaviest horse was used for fighting and in tournaments. The quickest was used for long journeys. The third carried the bags!

Knight and his horse

Dying for love!

Jaufre Rudel was a French knight. He sent love letters to the beautiful Countess of Tripoli, even though had never seen her! When he finally met her he fell into her arms and died!

Squire

What was dubbing?

A new knight was given a special ceremony called a dubbing. First, he had to spend a whole night in church, praying on his knees. Then the new knight was tapped on the shoulder with a sword.

Did knights fight with a ball?

Morning star

Knights hit the enemy with a spiked ball on a long chain. This was called a 'morning star'.

Knights used swords, too. Foot knights from Switzerland used a halberd. This was an axe with a hook on the back. It was good for getting a knight off his horse!

Sword

Get to the point!
Soldiers called 'retrievers' fetched all the fallen arrows. They had to run through the battle to get them!

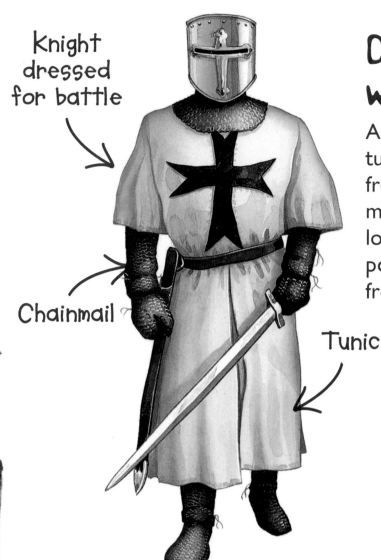

Knight dressed for battle

Chainmail

Tunic

Did knights wear woolly jumpers?

A knight in early times wore a bright tunic with long sleeves. It was made from wool or linen. He also wore metal armour called chainmail. It looked and felt like knitted wire! A padded jacket stopped the chainmail from scratching the skin.

Design

In later times, knights wore steel armour. They even wore metal shoes! Design your own suit of armour to protect a knight.

How long was the Hundred Years War?

The Hundred Years War was fought between the English and the French. It actually lasted for 116 years, between 1337 and 1453. English and Welsh soldiers used longbows against the French. The bowmen could fire 12 arrows every minute!

How were knights told apart?

A knight wore a helmet that covered his head. Even his soldiers could not recognize him! Each knight put a special symbol on his shield and robes. The symbols and colours were called a 'coat of arms'.

Don't shoot the messenger!

Using a coat of arms was called 'heraldry'. This is because the lord's messenger was called a 'herald'. The herald wore his lord's coat of arms as he crossed the battlefield.

Knight wearing coat of arms

What was a herald?

A herald was a messenger. He carried messages for knights during battles. The herald had to be able recognize each knight by his coat of arms. The heralds were very good at recognizing coats of arms. This eventually came to be known as heraldry.

Herald →

← Horse wearing coat of arms

Where did soldiers meet?

Each lord had a banner with his coat of arms on it. Knights and soldiers gathered around the banner on the battlefield. The lord could then explain his battle plans. The winner of a battle often stole the enemy's banner from him.

Make

Draw and cut out a shield from cardboard. Paint your own symbol on it.

Were castles cosy?

Castles were very cold and windy. The windows had wooden shutters but no glass. People wove thick, rich carpets and tapestries to hang on the walls. This made the castle warmer and brighter. Later castles had glass windows.

Design

Design and colour a patterned carpet for a cold castle wall. Use squared paper to get a repeat pattern.

Chapel tower

Bedroom

Garden

Were castles busy?

A castle was very busy. It had workshops, a flour mill, stables, dog kennels, a chapel, a blacksmith's and much more. People even grew their own fruit and vegetables in the castle grounds.

Prison tower

Smelly castles!

Castles were not swept very often. The floors were made from hard earth and covered with long grass from the river. Old food, rubbish and mess from cats and dogs was thrown on top. Herbs helped stop the smell!

Did castles have toilets?

Toilets were called 'garderobes'. They had wooden seats. Some were built into a thick wall. Others were built over a long pipe, or chute. The chute carried all the waste into the moat around the castle. The smell must have been awful!

Main gate

Where did lords and ladies shop?

Towns grew up around castles. Townspeople set up market stalls and workshops. They sold food, drink, clothing and tools to passing lords, ladies and knights.

Who collected the rubbish?

There were not any street sweepers! The rubbish and waste water were thrown into gutters. Animal bones, skin and rotting vegetables covered the cobbles and gravel. Rats ran around freely. Only heavy rain washed away the filth.

Awful art!

Builders carved monster faces on churches. The faces were carved at the end of gutters. These ugly monsters were called 'gargoyles'.

Knight and his squire

What did people die from?

Most people died from disease and hunger. In 1348, the Black Death disease killed millions of people in the British Isles. Flea bites from rats spread the disease. It was also spread by coughing and touching.

Create

Make a map of a town with a castle on it. The town will need a church, shops, and a market place. It will also need water and roads.

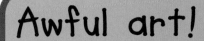

Did knights have fun?

Yes they did! Knights took part in competitions called tournaments. These helped them to improve their fighting. The knights formed two teams that fought each other in pretend battles.

Did knights only fight on horseback?

At a tournament, knights also fought on the ground. They wore heavy armour. Skill and speed were much more important than strength.

Make

Write and design a programme for a tournament. You can include fighting competitions and entertainment.

Rotten cheat!

Some knights tried to cheat in a jousting competition. They wore special armour that was fixed to the horse's saddle!

Knight taking part in a tournament

Jousting knight

How did knights find a wife?

Ladies from the king's court went to tournaments. The knights showed off their bravery to their favourite lady. Each knight tried to push another knight off his horse with a long pole called a lance. This was called jousting.

What was a siege?

People sometimes became trapped inside a castle if the enemy surrounded it. This was called a siege. The people inside could not get food supplies. So they had a terrible choice. They could either starve to death or surrender to the enemy.

Castle under attack

Think

Try to think of ways to get into a castle without being seen. Look at the castle on page 18 to help you find a way in. Draw a map of your route.

How did the castle crumble?

Sometimes the enemy bashed down the castle gates with battering rams. These were thick tree trunks capped with iron. The enemy also tried to climb the walls with giant ladders. Huge catapults hurled burning wood and stones.

Battering ram

Siege

Hairy weapons!

Giant catapults were wound up with ropes made of human hair! The hair was made into plaits and was very strong.

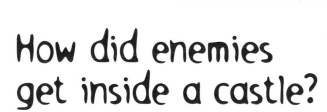

How did enemies get inside a castle?

Sometimes enemy soldiers dug tunnels underneath the castle. They then popped up inside the castle walls. The enemy also pushed wooden towers against the castle walls. Soldiers hiding in the towers leapt out and climbed into the castle.

What stopped the enemy?

Portcullis

Drawbridge

The drawbridge was pulled up. This stopped the enemy crossing the moat. Then people inside the castle lowered a heavy iron grate called a portcullis. This was like a metal gate behind the drawbridge.

Fire away!

Archers fired arrows at the enemy from the gaps at the top of the castle walls. These gaps were called battlements.

What were hot weapons?

Defenders stood on wooden platforms high on the castle walls. From here they poured boiling water onto the enemy below. They also poured down a burning chemical called quicklime.

Hot water was poured over enemies

What gave the enemy a surprise?

Castles were full of secret tunnels and hidden gates. Defending soldiers sometimes crept through them at night. When they got outside, they attacked the enemy as they slept.

Remember

Everybody in the castle tried to defend it. Can you remember all the kinds of people who lived in the castle?

Who was the bravest knight?

Saint George killed a dragon! The dragon was eating the people of Lydia, in Turkey. The king tried to stop the dragon by giving his daughter to it. A brave English knight called George killed the dragon when the people became Christians. The princess was saved and George became a saint.

Write

Who do you think was the bravest knight? Many knights wrote poetry. Try to write a poem about your favourite knight.

Saint George and the dragon

Joan of Arc

Who was Joan of Arc?

Joan of Arc was a young French girl. She gathered an army to fight the English who had surrounded the French city of Orleans. Joan and her army defeated the English, but later she was caught. She was accused of being a witch and was burned to death.

Expensive knight!

Many knights were captured in battle. Their families had to pay a lot of money to the enemy to set the knights free.

What happened to Sir Lancelot?

Arthur was a great king. Sir Lancelot was one of his best and bravest knights. However, Lancelot loved King Arthur's wife, Guinevere. The king found out and sent Lancelot away.

Quiz time

Do you remember what you have read about knights and castles? These questions will test your memory. The pictures will help you. If you get stuck, read the pages again.

1. Why were castles built on hills?

page 4

2. What was a moat?

page 5

3. Who were the barons?

page 11

4. What happened at knight school?

page 12

5. What was dubbing?

page 13

6. Did knights wear woolly jumpers?

page 15

7. Where did soldiers meet?

page 17

8. Where did lords and ladies shop?

page 20

9. What did people die from?

page 21

10. How did a knight find a wife?

page 23

11. How did the castle crumble?

page 25

12. Who was Joan of Arc?

page 29

13. What happened to Sir Lancelot?

page 29

Answers

1. So people could see the enemy
2. A watery ditch around a castle
3. The most powerful noblemen
4. Boys were trained to be knights
5. A special ceremony for a new knight
6. No, they wore chainmail and tunics
7. On the battlefield
8. At market stalls and workshops
9. From disease, the Black Death
10. When he was jousting
11. The walls were bashed with battering rams
12. A French girl who defeated the English
13. He was sent away by King Arthur

Index